ENGLISH TOWN

FOR EVERYONE

BOOK 1

Contents

Characters

Teddy's Dad

Teddy's Mom

Teddy

Rachel's Dad

Rachel's Mom

Rachel

Chris

Hello Song

Hello, everyone.
Hello, teacher!
Hello, friends!

Let's have fun together.
We'll have a good time.

Are you ready to start?
We're ready!

Here we go!

Goodbye Song

Did you have fun?

It's time to say goodbye.
See you next time!
See you next time!

Did you enjoy the class?
Yes! We had a fun time!
Yes! We had a fun time!

See you later! See you later!
Goodbye. Goodbye.

Bye! Bye!

Greetings

Let's Talk

A. Look, listen, and repeat.

B. Listen and practice.

Good morning.

morning   afternoon   evening   night

C. Listen, point, and say.

A: Good morning.
B: Good morning.

Let's Learn

A. Listen and chant.

Good afternoon.

Good afternoon.

Saturday, Saturday.

It's Saturday.

Oh, it's camping day.

Fun, fun. We had fun.

Good night.

Good night.

B. Look, read, and choose.

1

Good morning.

2

It's Saturday.

3

Good evening.

4

Good night.

a Good night.
b Good evening.
c Oh, it's camping day.
d Good morning.

C. Match and say.

A: Good morning.
B: Good morning.

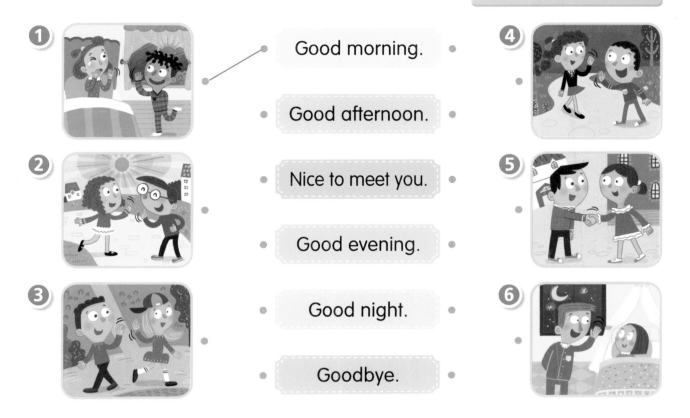

① Good morning.

Good afternoon.

② Nice to meet you.

Good evening.

③ Good night.

Goodbye.

④

⑤

⑥

D. Work with your friends.

- Look at the time in each city on the map and write each greeting. Then, do a role-play.

Good morning. Good morning.

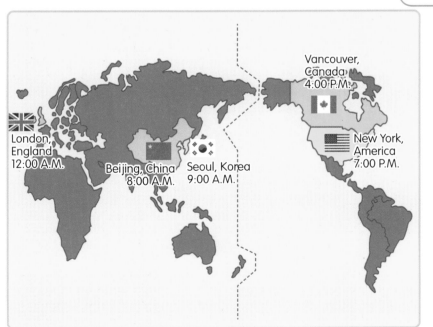

Korea	Good morning.
China	
Canada	
America	
England	

Lesson 2 Breakfast

Let's Talk

A. Look, listen, and repeat.

B. Listen and practice.

We have cereal.

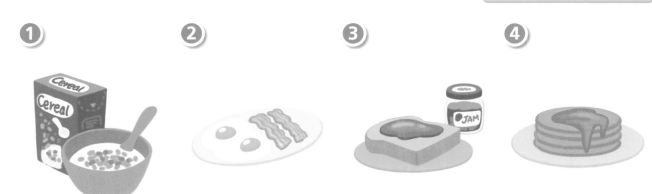

①	②	③	④
cereal	bacon and eggs	bread and jam	pancakes

C. Listen, point, and say.

A: What's for breakfast?
B: We have bread and jam.

Let's Learn

A. Listen and chant.

What's the weather like today?

It's sunny.

What's for breakfast?

We have bacon and eggs.

We have bacon and eggs.

What's for breakfast?

We have pancakes.

We have pancakes.

B. Look, listen, and match.

1

2

3

C. Check, ask, and answer.

> A: What's for breakfast?
> B: We have pancakes.

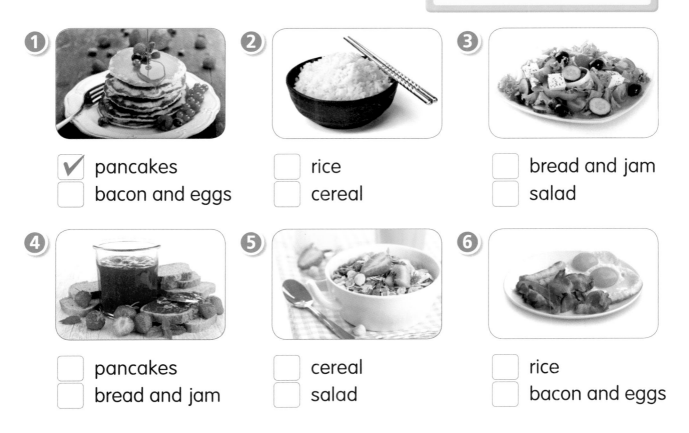

1. ☑ pancakes
   ☐ bacon and eggs

2. ☐ rice
   ☐ cereal

3. ☐ bread and jam
   ☐ salad

4. ☐ pancakes
   ☐ bread and jam

5. ☐ cereal
   ☐ salad

6. ☐ rice
   ☐ bacon and eggs

D. Work with your friends.

- Draw your family's breakfast and do a role-play.

Example

We have bacon and eggs.

3 What's for Breakfast?

A. Listen and repeat the story.

B. Listen and number the pictures.

Dodo

Dodo's Dad

Dodo's Mom

C. Read and check True or False.

1   It's rainy today.   True ☐   False ☐

2   Dodo's birthday is on Saturday.   True ☐   False ☐

3   Dodo's family eats pancakes for breakfast.   True ☐   False ☐

D. Choose what you want to eat for breakfast and do a role-play.

 ☐

 ☐

 ☐

Let's Play

A. Listen and sing.

We Have Cereal

Oh, it's camping day.
What's the weather like today?
　It's sunny.
What's for breakfast?
　We have cereal.

Oh, it's camping day.
What's the weather like today?
　It's sunny.
What's for breakfast?
　We have bread and jam.

B. Play a board game.

★ Good _____.
　- Good _____.

♥ What's for breakfast?
　- We have _____.

16

Breakfasts around the World

In France, toast with jam and croissants are common for breakfast. People eat them with coffee or juice.

The famous American breakfast is thick pancakes with syrup and blueberries. People eat them with bacon.

Congee, a type of rice porridge, is a popular breakfast in China. People eat it plain or with ground meat.

Check It Out!
1. Do people around the world eat the same food for breakfast?
2. What is the famous breakfast in America?

Lesson 4 Packing

Let's Talk

A. Look, listen, and repeat.

Get dressed.

Okay.

Did you pack your pants?

Yes, I did.

ACT IT OUT

Okay.

B. Listen and practice.

Did you pack your pants?

① pants ② socks ③ underwear ④ shirt

C. Listen, point, and say.

A: Did you pack your socks?
B: Yes, I did.

Let's Learn

A. Listen and chant.

Oh, it's camping day.

Get dressed. Get dressed.

Okay. Okay.

Pants, pants.

Did you pack your pants?

Yes, I did.

Underwear, underwear.

Did you pack your underwear?

Yes, I did.

B. Look, listen, and number the pictures.

C. Go down the ladder.
Then, ask and answer.

A: Did you pack your socks?
B: Yes, I did.

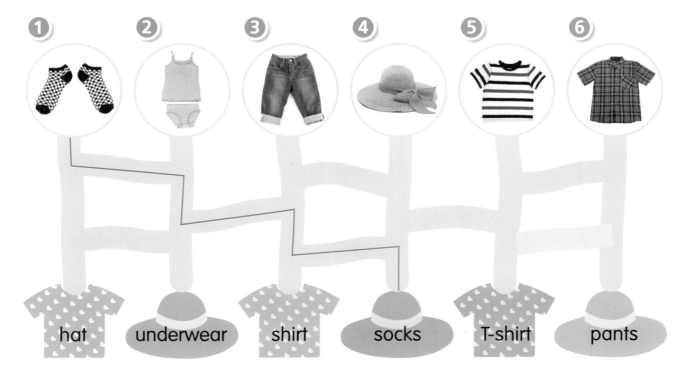

① ② ③ ④ ⑤ ⑥

hat   underwear   shirt   socks   T-shirt   pants

D. Work with your friends.

- Ask your partner what he/she packed to go camping and color the items.

Did you pack your underwear?

Yes, I did.

Lesson 5 Outdoor Activities

Let's Talk

A. Look, listen, and repeat.

B. Listen and practice.

Do you like camping?

① camping ② in-line skating ③ hiking ④ fishing

C. Listen, point, and say.

A: Do you like camping?
B: Yes, I love camping.

Let's Learn

A. Listen and chant.

Sorry for being late.

It's not a problem.

Do you like hiking?

Yes. Yes, I love hiking.

Sorry for being late.

It's not a problem.

Do you like fishing?

Yes. Yes, I love fishing.

B. Look, read, and circle.

1

Do you like (in-line skating / camping)?

Yes, I love (in-line skating / camping).

2

Do you like (hiking / fishing)?

Yes, I love (hiking / fishing).

3

Do you like (camping / fishing)?

Yes, I love (camping / fishing).

C. Check, ask, and answer.

> A: Do you like fishing?
> B: Yes, I love fishing.

1
- ✔ fishing
- ☐ running

2
- ☐ fishing
- ☐ hiking

3
- ☐ hiking
- ☐ jumping rope

4
- ☐ camping
- ☐ in-line skating

5
- ☐ camping
- ☐ jumping rope

6
- ☐ running
- ☐ in-line skating

D. Work with your friends.

- Write the outdoor activities you like to do and ask your partner if he/she likes to do them, too. Then, write down the activities he/she likes to do.

Do you like hiking?

Yes, I love hiking.

You	Your Friend
1. hiking	1. _____
2. _____	2. _____
3. _____	3. _____
4. _____	4. _____

6 I Love In-line Skating

A. Listen and repeat the story.

B. Listen and number the pictures.

Rubi

Sorry for being late.

It's not a problem.

Did you pack your socks?

Yes, I did.

C. Read and choose.

1 What does Dodo love?

a He loves camping. **b** He loves in-line skating.

2 Did Dodo pack his socks?

a Yes, he did. **b** No, he didn't.

D. Choose which outdoor activity you want to do and do a role-play.

Let's Play

A. Listen and sing.

I Love Camping

Get dressed.

  Okay. Okay.

Did you pack your socks?

  Yes, I did.

Do you like camping?

  Yes, I love camping.

Get dressed.

  Okay. Okay.

Did you pack your shirt?

  Yes, I did.

Do you like in-line skating?

  Yes, I love in-line skating.

B. Play a board game.

♥ Do you like _____?
- Yes, I love _____.

★ Did you pack your _____?
- Yes, I did.

The Difference between In-line Skating and Ice Skating

Each in-line skate has four wheels in a line. But each ice skate has a blade. You can in-line skate inside on rinks or outside on hard ground. You can ice skate inside on rinks or outside on frozen lakes. Do you like in-line skating or ice skating?

Check It Out!

1. What is the difference between in-line skates and ice skates?
2. Where do you in-line skate and ice skate?

7 Camping Items

Let's Talk

A. Look, listen, and repeat.

B. Listen and practice.

I brought an(a) umbrella.

① umbrella

② raincoat

③ garden spade

④ flashlight

C. Listen, point, and say.

A: What did you bring?
B: I brought a(an) flashlight.

Let's Learn

A. Listen and chant.

We're here. We're here.
Hooray! Hooray!
What did you bring?
Umbrella, umbrella. I brought an umbrella.

We're here. We're here.
Hooray! Hooray!
What did you bring?
Raincoat, raincoat. I brought a raincoat.

B. Look, read, and check.

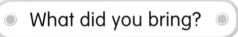 What did you bring?

1

☐ I brought a flashlight.
☐ I brought a raincoat.

2

☐ I brought a ball.
☐ I brought a garden spade.

3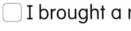

☐ I brought a raincoat.
☐ I brought a jump rope.

4

☐ I brought a flashlight.
☐ I brought an umbrella.

C. Choose, ask, and answer.

> A: What did you bring?
> B: I brought a(an) flashlight.

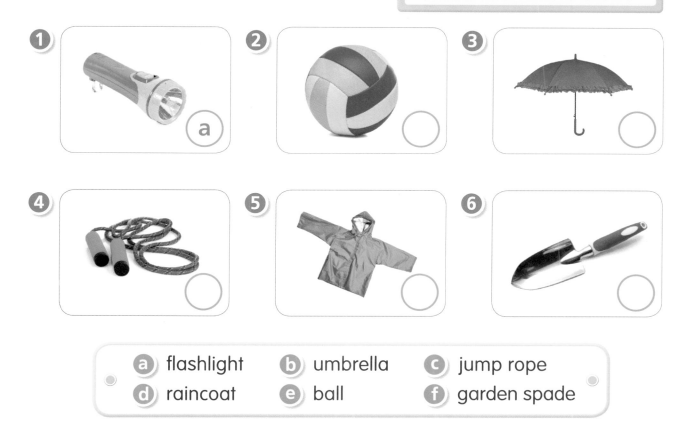

① a

②

③

④

⑤

⑥

a flashlight   b umbrella   c jump rope
d raincoat   e ball   f garden spade

D. Work with your friends.

- Find six camping items in the picture and do a role-play.

8 Belongings

Let's Talk

A. Look, listen, and repeat.

B. **Listen and practice.**

Don't worry. You can use my blanket.

①   ②   ③   ④

blanket   pillow   shampoo   toothpaste

C. **Listen, point, and say.**

A: Don't worry. You can use my pillow.
B: Thank you.

Let's Learn

A. Listen and chant.

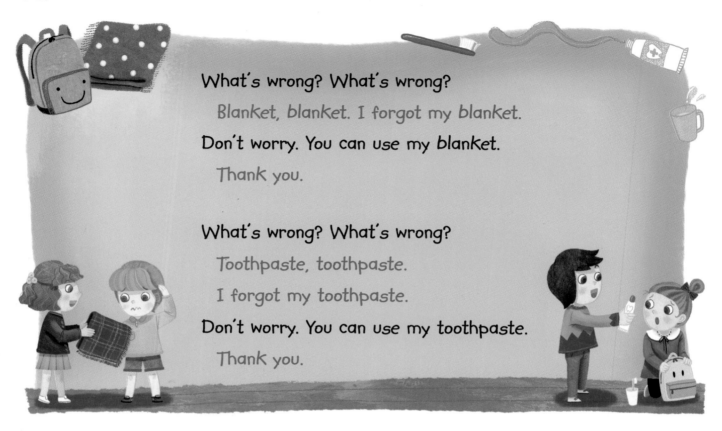

What's wrong? What's wrong?

Blanket, blanket. I forgot my blanket.

Don't worry. You can use my blanket.

Thank you.

What's wrong? What's wrong?

Toothpaste, toothpaste.

I forgot my toothpaste.

Don't worry. You can use my toothpaste.

Thank you.

B. Look, listen, and choose.

1. a   b
2. a   b
3. a   b
4. a   b

C. Match and say.

> A: Don't worry. You can use my shampoo.
> B: Thank you.

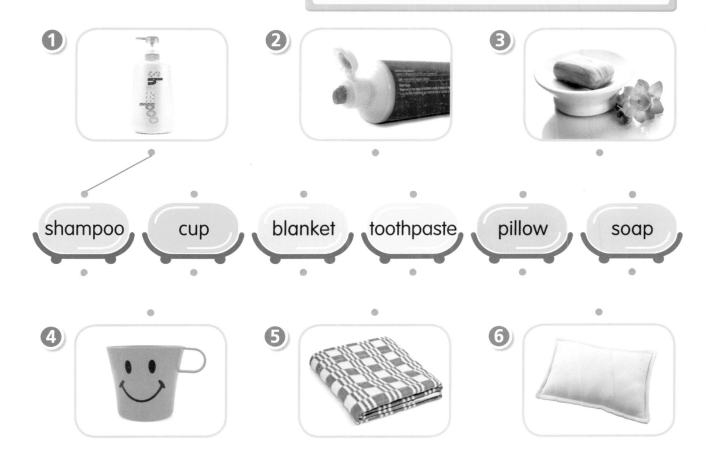

1 **2** **3**

shampoo　　cup　　blanket　　toothpaste　　pillow　　soap

4 **5** **6**

D. Work with your friends.

- Suppose your partner forgot things to bring. Choose A or B and do a role-play.

A

Don't worry. You can use my toothpaste.

Thank you.

B

9 You Can Use My Pillow

A. Listen and repeat the story.

B. Listen and number the pictures.

Roy

What's wrong?

I forgot my pillow.

Don't worry. You can use my pillow.

Thank you.

C. Read and match.

1 Where did Roy and Bebe go? •

• ⓐ They went to Dodo's house.
• ⓑ They went to a park.

2 What did Bebe forget? •

• ⓐ He forgot his blanket.
• ⓑ He forgot his pillow.

D. Choose what you brought to a pajama party and do a role-play.

Let's Play

A. Listen and sing.

What Did You Bring?

We're here.
Hooray!
What did you bring?
I brought a flashlight.
What did you bring?
I brought a garden spade.

What's wrong?
I forgot my shampoo.
You can use my shampoo.
I forgot my pillow.
You can use my pillow.
Thank you. Thank you.

B. Play tic-tac-toe.

★ What did you bring?
  - I brought a(an) _____.

♥ Don't worry. You can use my _____.
  - Thank you.

Pajama Parties

When you go to a pajama party, you stay overnight at the home of a friend. You need pajamas to wear at night. Don't forget some snacks. You can play board games and watch movies with your friends. Now, let's have fun at a pajama party. Hooray!

Check It Out!

1. What do you need for a pajama party?
2. What can you do at a pajama party?

1. Listening

A. Listen and check.

1

a. ☐
b. ☐

2

a. ☐
b. ☐

3

a. ☐
b. ☐

4

a. ☐
b. ☐

5

a. ☐
b. ☐

6

a. ☐
b. ☐

B. Listen and answer the questions.

1 What day is it?
a. It's hiking day.
b. It's fishing day.
c. It's camping day.

2 What did Jina bring?
a. an umbrella   b. a raincoat   c. a flashlight

A. Look, listen, and reply.

①

②

③

④

B. Number the sentences in order and talk with your partner.

◯ Don't worry.
   You can use my blanket.

① What's wrong?

◯ I forgot my blanket.

◯ Thank you.

A. Read and match.

1. What did you bring? •   • a. Yes, I love fishing.

2. What's the weather like today? •   • b. Thank you.

3. Don't worry. You can use my toothpaste. •   • c. It's sunny.

4. What's for breakfast? •   • d. Yes, I did.

5. Do you like fishing? •   • e. I brought a flashlight.

6. Did you pack your socks? •   • f. We have bacon and eggs.

B. Read and check True or False.

In France, toast with jam and croissants are common for breakfast. People eat them with coffee or juice.

The famous American breakfast is thick pancakes with syrup and blueberries. People eat them with bacon.

Congee, a type of rice porridge, is a popular breakfast in China. People eat it plain or with ground meat.

1. Croissants are a common breakfast in France. .... True ☐ False ☐

2. The famous American breakfast is blueberry cake. ...... True ☐ False ☐

3. In China, people eat congee with ground meat. .... True ☐ False ☐

44

4. Writing

e-learning

A. Write the words.

> underwear   raincoat   pancakes
> in-line skating   pillow   fishing

1

_____

2

_____

3

_____

4

_____

5

I brought a
_____ .

6

I love
_____ .

B. Write the answers.

1 A: What's for breakfast?

B: _____

(bacon and eggs / have / we / .)

2 A: What's wrong?

B: _____

(my / forgot / I / blanket / .)

3 A: What did you bring?

B: _____

(a / brought / I / flashlight / .)

11 Going Places

Let's Talk

A. Look, listen, and repeat.

B. Listen and practice.

We're going to the river.

① river

② sea

③ mountains

④ cave

A: Where are we going?
B: We're going to the cave.

C. Listen, point, and say.

Let's Learn

A. Listen and chant.

Let's go fishing.

Great, great. Sounds great.

Where are we going?

We're going to the sea.

We're going to the sea.

Where are we going?

We're going to the mountains.

We're going to the mountains.

B. Look, read, and match.

Where are we going?

1 We're going to the cave.

2 We're going to the sea.

3 We're going to the river.

4 We're going to the mountains.

e-learning

C. Choose, ask, and answer.

> A: Where are we going?
> B: We're going to the river.

1 — c

2 — ◯

3 — ◯

4 — ◯

5 — ◯

6 — ◯

- a mountains
- b cave
- c river
- d park
- e zoo
- f sea

D. Work with your friends.

- Go through the maze and then do a role-play.

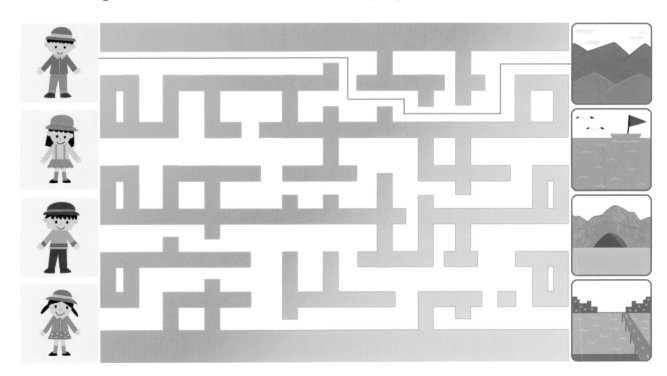

12 Fishing

Let's Talk

A. Look, listen, and repeat.

ACT IT **OUT**

B. Listen and practice.

This lemon is bigger than that one.

① lemon, bigger   **②** orange, smaller   **③** peach, heavier   **④** pear, lighter

C. Listen, point, and say.

A: This ham is lighter than that one.
B: Yes, it is.

Let's Learn

A. Listen and chant.

I caught one.

I caught one, too.

This fish is heavier than that one.

Yes, yes. Yes, it is.

I caught one.

I caught one, too.

This fish is lighter than that one.

Yes, yes. Yes, it is.

B. Look, listen, and check True or False.

1 True ☐ False ☐

2 True ☐ False ☐

3 True ☐ False ☐

4 True ☐ False ☐

C. Check and say.

A: This ball is bigger than that one.
B: Yes, it is.

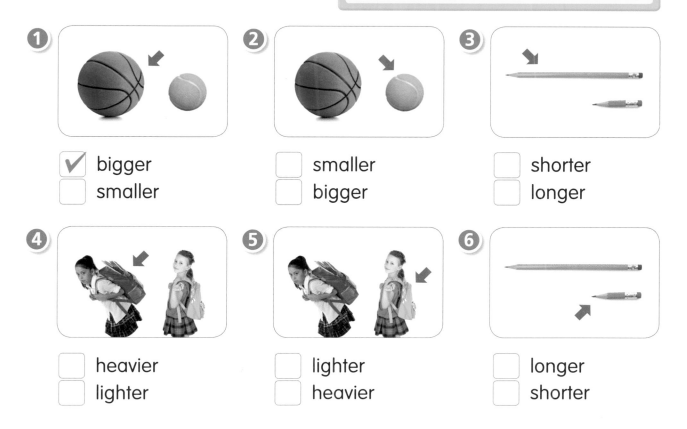

1 ☑ bigger
☐ smaller

2 ☐ smaller
☐ bigger

3 ☐ shorter
☐ longer

4 ☐ heavier
☐ lighter

5 ☐ lighter
☐ heavier

6 ☐ longer
☐ shorter

D. Work with your friends.

- Find things to compare in your classroom and describe them below.

This pencil case is smaller than that one.

Yes, it is.

1 This pencil case is smaller than that one.

2 This _____ is _____ than that one.

3 This _____ is _____ than that one.

Lesson 13 Let's Go Fishing

A. Listen and repeat the story.

B. Listen and number the pictures.

54

Bebe's Dad

I caught one.

I caught one, too.

This fish is bigger than that one.

Yes, it is.

C. Read and choose.

1 What are Bebe and Dodo doing?

a hiking **b** fishing **c** camping

2 Where are Bebe and Dodo going?

a the cave **b** the mountains **c** the sea

D. Choose the place you want to go to and do a role-play.

Let's Play

A. Listen and sing.

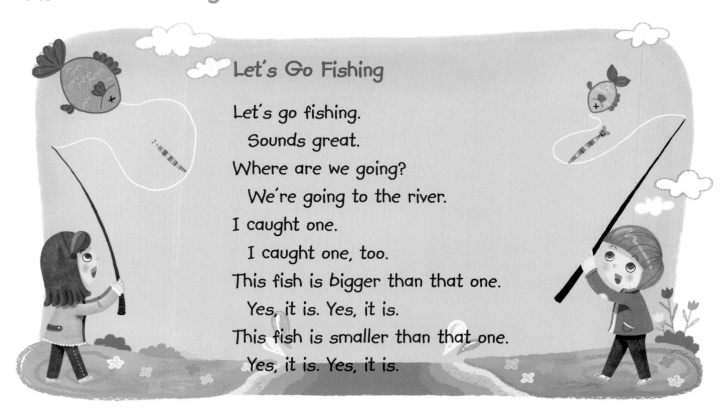

Let's Go Fishing

Let's go fishing.
  Sounds great.
Where are we going?
  We're going to the river.
I caught one.
  I caught one, too.
This fish is bigger than that one.
  Yes, it is. Yes, it is.
This fish is smaller than that one.
  Yes, it is. Yes, it is.

B. Play bingo.

sea
zoo
cave
park
river
mountains

sea

bigger
smaller
heavier
lighter
longer
shorter

A Fun Water Sport: Snorkeling

Do you like going to the sea? You can enjoy many water sports there. Snorkeling is one of them. You can see amazing sea life under the sea. You can take pictures of beautiful fish. For snorkeling, you need a diving mask and fins. You should do warm-up exercises before doing it.

Now, let's dive into the sea!

Check It Out!

1. What can you see when you snorkel?
2. What things do you need for snorkeling?

14 Games

Let's Talk

A. Look, listen, and repeat.

B. Listen and practice.

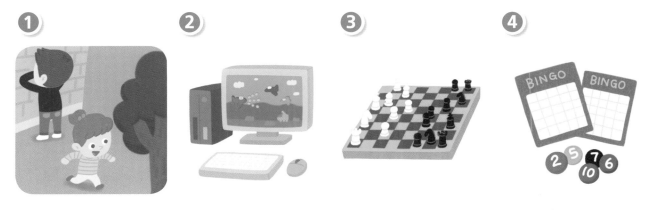

① hide and seek ② a computer game ③ chess ④ bingo

C. Listen, point, and say.

A: What would you like to play?
B: Let's play bingo.

Let's Learn

A. Listen and chant.

Dad, play with us.

Okay, okay.

What, what? What would you like to play?

Let's play a computer game.

Mom, play with us.

Okay, okay.

What, what? What would you like to play?

Let's play chess.

B. Look, listen, and number the pictures.

e-learning

C. Go down the ladder.
Then, ask and answer.

A: What would you like to play?
B: Let's play a computer game.

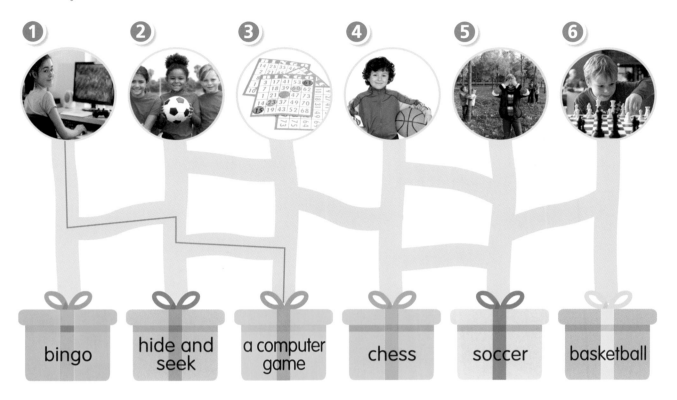

① ② ③ ④ ⑤ ⑥

bingo | hide and seek | a computer game | chess | soccer | basketball

D. Work with your friends.

- Write down what you want to play and then do a role-play with your friends. Write down their answers.

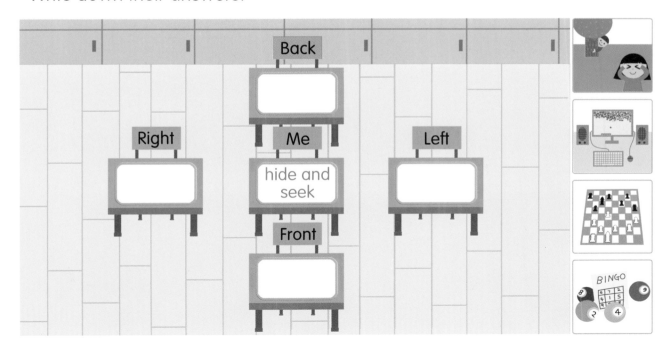

15 Dinnertime

Let's Talk

A. Look, listen, and repeat.

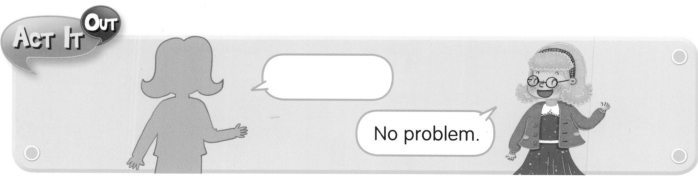

B. Listen and practice.

Be careful using the knife.

① ② ③ ④

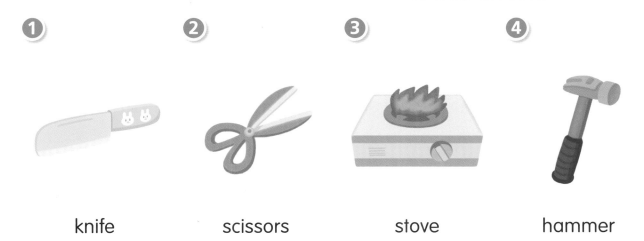

knife   scissors   stove   hammer

C. Listen, point, and say.

A: Be careful using the knife.
B: Okay, I will. Thanks.

Let's Learn

A. Listen and chant.

It's dinnertime. Yeah!

Will you help me with dinner?

No problem. No problem.

Be careful using the scissors.

Okay, I will. Thanks.

Be careful using the knife.

Okay, I will. Thanks.

B. Look, read, and check.

1

☐ Be careful using the hammer.
☐ Be careful using the scissors.

2

☐ Where are we going?
☐ Will you help me with dinner?

3

☐ Be careful using the knife.
☐ Be careful using the scissors.

4

☐ Be careful using the stove.
☐ Be careful using the hammer.

C. Match and say.

> A: Be careful using the hammer.
> B: Okay, I will. Thanks.

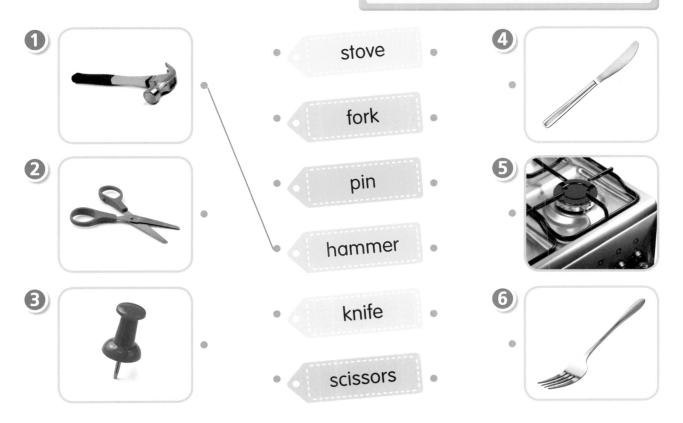

1

stove

fork

pin

hammer

knife

scissors

4

5

6

2

3

D. Work with your friends.

- Do a role-play about what they should use carefully in each picture and circle it.

Be careful using the hammer.

16 Will You Help Me with Dinner?

A. Listen and repeat the story.

B. Listen and number the pictures.

○ ○ ○ ○

C. Read and check True or False.

1 Rubi should be careful using the knife.　　True ☐　False ☐

2 Rubi wants to play a computer game.　　True ☐　False ☐

D. Choose what you want to play and do a role-play.

 ☐  ☐  ☐

A. Listen and sing.

Let's Play Together

Play with us.
  What would you like to play?
Let's play hide and seek.
  Okay. Okay.

Will you help me with dinner?
  No problem. No problem.
Be careful using the stove.
  Okay, I will. Thanks.

B. Play a board game.

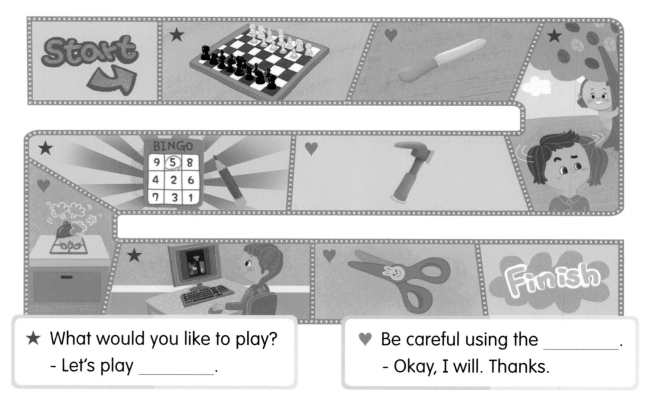

★ What would you like to play?
  - Let's play _____.

♥ Be careful using the _____.
  - Okay, I will. Thanks.

Domino Toppling

Do you know about domino toppling? It's easy to do. First, set up a line of dominoes. Second, tap the first domino. The dominoes will fall down in order. Be careful not to knock down any dominoes when you make lines. Start with a simple line of dominoes. Then, try harder designs like circles. You can make various domino designs.

Now, let's topple some dominoes!

Check It Out!

1. What should we do first when we want to topple dominoes?
2. What should we be careful not to do?

17 Campfire

Let's Talk

A. Look, listen, and repeat.

ACT IT OUT

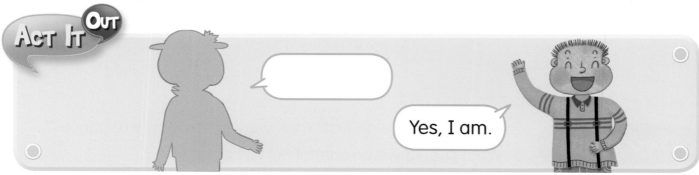

B. Listen and practice.

Could you play the harmonica?

①

harmonica

② trumpet

③ tambourine

④ xylophone

C. Listen, point, and say.

A: Could you play the trumpet?
B: Sure, why not?

A. Listen and chant.

Are you excited?

Yes, I am. Yes, I am.

Could you play the xylophone?

Sure, why not?

Are you excited?

Yes, I am. Yes, I am.

Could you play the trumpet?

Sure, why not?

B. Look, read, and match.

1 Could you play the ? •   • xylophone

2 Could you play the  ? •   • harmonica

3 Could you play the  ? •   • tambourine

4 Could you play the ? •   • trumpet

e-learning

C. Check, ask, and answer.

A: Could you play the tambourine?
B: Sure, why not?

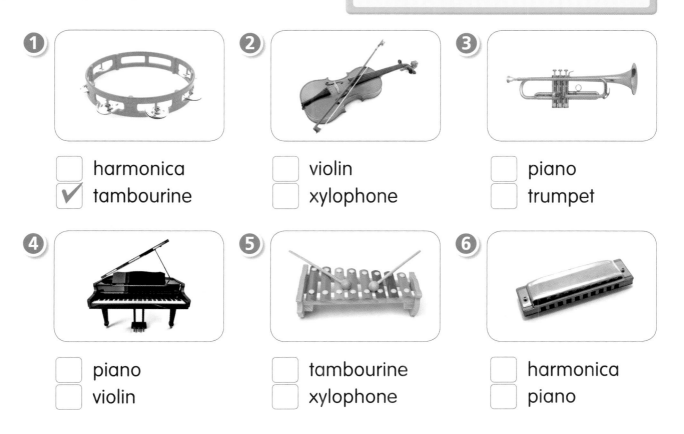

① ☐ harmonica
☑ tambourine

② ☐ violin
☐ xylophone

③ ☐ piano
☐ trumpet

④ ☐ piano
☐ violin

⑤ ☐ tambourine
☐ xylophone

⑥ ☐ harmonica
☐ piano

D. Work with your friends.

- Write some instruments below and then ask your partner to play them by miming.

Could you play the violin?

Sure, why not?

Instruments
1. violin
2.
3.
4.
5.

18 Shooting Star

Let's Talk

A. Look, listen, and repeat.

ACT IT OUT

B. Listen and practice.

> My wish is to get a new **bike**.

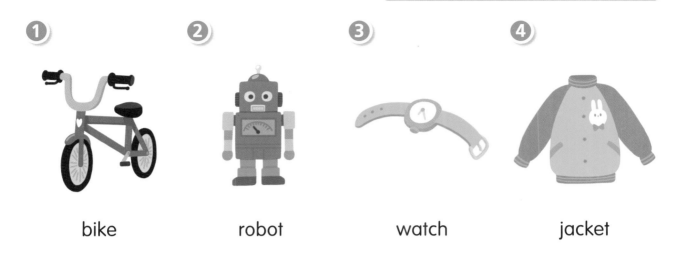

① bike

② robot

③ watch

④ jacket

> A: Let's make a wish.
> B: My wish is to get a new **robot**.

C. Listen, point, and say.

Let's Learn

A. Listen and chant.

Look at the shooting star.

Amazing! Amazing!

Let's make a wish.

Sounds great.

What did you wish for?

I can't tell you.

Come on. Tell me.

Alright. My wish is to get a new robot.

B. Look, listen, and choose.

1 a b

2 a b

3 a b

4 a b

e-learning

C. Choose and say.

A: Let's make a wish.
B: My wish is to get a new jacket.

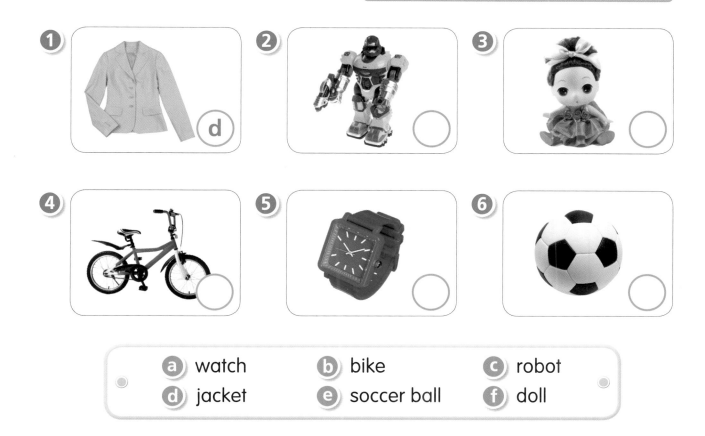

① d
② ○
③ ○
④ ○
⑤ ○
⑥ ○

- **a** watch **b** bike **c** robot
- **d** jacket **e** soccer ball **f** doll

D. Work with your friends.

- Write down two more wishes on the wish list and then do a role-play.

Wish List

1 My wish is to get a new doll.
2
3

19 Are You Excited?

A. Listen and repeat the story.

B. Listen and number the pictures.

C. **Read and correct the sentences.**

1 Dodo is sad.

2 Dodo's wish is to get a new tambourine.

3 Dodo can't play the violin.

D. **Choose the thing that you want to get and do a role-play.**

Let's Play

A. Listen and sing.

Let's Make a Wish

Are you excited?
　Yes, yes. Yes, I am.
Look at the shooting star.
　Wow! Amazing!
Let's make a wish.
　My wish is to get a new harmonica.
Could you play the harmonica?
　Sure, why not?

B. Play a quick reading game.

8. Amazing!

1. Are you excited?

7. Look at the shooting star.

2. Could you play the trumpet?

6. My wish is to get a new robot.

3. My wish is to get a new bike.

5. Could you play the tambourine?

4. Let's make a wish.

Shooting Stars

Have you ever seen shooting stars in the sky? They look like stars moving across the sky. But, actually, they are different from normal stars. A shooting star is a small piece of rock or dust. When it falls down, it is hot and glowing. Most shooting stars don't reach the ground. They burn up in the air. Unlike shooting stars, normal stars don't fall and burn up quickly.

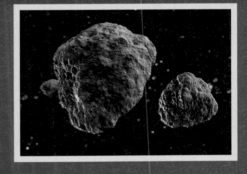

Check It Out!

1. Why are shooting stars different from normal stars?
2. Do shooting stars usually reach the ground? Why or why not?

20 Assessment Test 2

1. Listening

A. Listen and check.

①

a. ☐
b. ☐

②

a. ☐
b. ☐

③
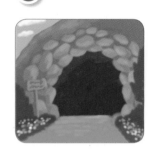
a. ☐
b. ☐

④

a. ☐
b. ☐

⑤

a. ☐
b. ☐

⑥

a. ☐
b. ☐

B. Listen and answer the questions.

① Where are they going?
   a. They are going to the sea.
   b. They are going to the river.
   c. They are going to the mountains.

② What would Tom like to play?
   a. chess   b. bingo   c. a computer game

A. Look, listen, and reply.

①

②

③

④

B. Number the sentences in order and talk with your partner.

◯   Yes, it is.

①   I caught one.

◯   This fish is bigger than that one.

◯   I caught one, too.

A. Read and match.

① Where are we going? •   • a. I caught one, too.

② I caught one. •   • b. Yes, I am.

③ Be careful using the knife. •   • c. We're going to the river.

④ Could you play the harmonica? •   • d. Amazing!

⑤ Look at the shooting star. •   • e. Okay, I will. Thanks.

⑥ Are you excited? •   • f. Sure, why not?

B. Read and check True or False.

Have you ever seen shooting stars in the sky? They look like stars moving across the sky. But, actually, they are different from normal stars. A shooting star is a small piece of rock or dust. When it falls down, it is hot and glowing. Most shooting stars don't reach the ground. They burn up in the air. Unlike shooting stars, normal stars don't fall and burn up quickly.

① Shooting stars are different from normal stars. .... True ☐   False ☐

② When shooting stars fall down, they are cold and glowing. .... True ☐   False ☐

③ Normal stars fall and burn up quickly. .... True ☐   False ☐

A. Write the words.

robot   smaller   bingo
mountains   xylophone   scissors

1

_____

2

_____

3

_____

4

_____

5

Could you play the

_____ ?

6

This orange is

_____

than that one.

B. Write the answers.

1 A: Where are we going?

B: _____

(we're / sea / to / going / the / .)

2 A: What would you like to play?

B: _____

(play / hide and seek / let's / .)

3 A: Let's make a wish.

B: _____

(new / get / wish / to / my / a / is / bike / .)

Syllabus

Lesson	Topic	Language	Key Vocabulary
Lesson 1	Greetings	Good morning. - Good morning. It's Saturday. - Oh, it's camping day.	morning afternoon evening night
Lesson 2	Breakfast	What's for breakfast? - We have cereal. What's the weather like today? - It's sunny.	cereal bacon and eggs bread and jam pancakes
Lesson 3	What's for Breakfast?	Step Up 1 (Review Lessons 1-2) *Reading Time: Breakfasts around the World	
Lesson 4	Packing	Did you pack your pants? - Yes, I did. Get dressed. - Okay.	pants socks underwear shirt
Lesson 5	Outdoor Activities	Do you like camping? - Yes, I love camping. Sorry for being late. - It's not a problem.	camping in-line skating hiking fishing
Lesson 6	I Love In-line Skating	Step Up 2 (Review Lessons 4-5) *Reading Time: The Difference between In-line Skating and Ice Skating	
Lesson 7	Camping Items	What did you bring? - I brought an umbrella. We're here. - Hooray!	umbrella raincoat garden spade flashlight
Lesson 8	Belongings	Don't worry. You can use my blanket. - Thank you. What's wrong? - I forgot my blanket.	blanket pillow shampoo toothpaste
Lesson 9	You Can Use My Pillow	Step Up 3 (Review Lessons 7-8) *Reading Time: Pajama Parties	
Lesson 10	Assessment Test 1 (Review Lessons 1-9)		

Lesson	Topic	Language	Key Vocabulary
Lesson 11	Going Places	Where are we going? - We're going to the river. Let's go fishing. - Sounds great.	river sea mountains cave
Lesson 12	Fishing	This fish is bigger than that one. - Yes, it is. I caught one. - I caught one, too.	bigger smaller heavier lighter
Lesson 13	Let's Go Fishing	Step Up 4 (Review Lessons 11-12) *Reading Time: A Fun Water Sport: Snorkeling	
Lesson 14	Games	What would you like to play? - Let's play hide and seek. Play with us. - Okay.	hide and seek a computer game chess bingo
Lesson 15	Dinnertime	Be careful using the knife. - Okay, I will. Thanks. Will you help me with dinner? - No problem.	knife scissors stove hammer
Lesson 16	Will You Help Me with Dinner?	Step Up 5 (Review Lessons 14-15) *Reading Time: Domino Toppling	
Lesson 17	Campfire	Could you play the harmonica? - Sure, why not? Are you excited? - Yes, I am.	harmonica trumpet tambourine xylophone
Lesson 18	Shooting Star	Let's make a wish. - My wish is to get a new bike. Look at the shooting star. - Amazing!	bike robot watch jacket
Lesson 19	Are You Excited?	Step Up 6 (Review Lessons 17-18) *Reading Time: Shooting Stars	
Lesson 20	Assessment Test 2 (Review Lessons 11-19)		

Flashcard List

morning		afternoon		evening	
night		cereal		bacon and eggs	
bread and jam		pancakes		pants	
socks		underwear		shirt	
camping		in-line skating		hiking	
fishing		umbrella		raincoat	
garden spade		flashlight		blanket	
pillow		shampoo		toothpaste	
river		sea		mountains	
cave		bigger		smaller	
heavier		lighter		hide and seek	
a computer game		chess		bingo	
knife		scissors		stove	
hammer		harmonica		trumpet	
tambourine		xylophone		bike	
robot		watch		jacket	

	Vocabulary	Meaning	Sentence
1	afternoon*	오후	Good afternoon.
2	camping	캠핑, 야영	Oh, it's camping day.
3	day	날, 하루	Oh, it's camping day.
4	evening*	저녁	Good evening.
5	goodbye*	안녕히 가세요, 작별 인사	Goodbye.
6	meet*	만나다	Nice to meet you.
7	morning*	아침	Good morning.
8	nice	(기분) 좋은, 즐거운	Nice to meet you.
9	night*	밤	Good night.
10	oh	오 (감탄하는 말)	Oh, it's camping day.
11	Saturday	토요일	It's Saturday.
12	you	너, 당신	Nice to meet you.

	Vocabulary	Meaning	Sentence
1	bacon and eggs*	베이컨 에그	We have bacon and eggs.
2	bread and jam*	잼 바른 빵	We have bread and jam.
3	breakfast	아침 식사	What's for breakfast?
4	cereal*	시리얼	We have cereal.
5	pancake*	팬케이크	We have pancakes.
6	rice*	쌀, 밥	We have rice.
7	salad*	샐러드	We have salad.
8	sunny	화창한	It's sunny.
9	today	오늘	What's the weather like today?
10	we	우리	We have cereal.
11	weather	날씨	What's the weather like today?
12	what	무엇	What's for breakfast?

	Vocabulary	Meaning	Sentence
1	camping*	캠핑, 야영	Do you like camping?
2	fishing*	낚시	Do you like fishing?
3	for	~에 대해	Sorry for being late.
4	hiking*	하이킹	Do you like hiking?
5	in-line skating*	인라인 스케이트	Do you like in-line skating?
6	jumping rope*	줄넘기	Do you like jumping rope?
7	late	늦은	Sorry for being late.
8	like	좋아하다	Do you like camping?
9	not	~아니다, 않다	It's not a problem.
10	problem	문제	It's not a problem.
11	running*	달리기	Do you like running?
12	sorry	미안한	Sorry for being late.

	Vocabulary	Meaning	Sentence
1	blade	(칼, 도구 등의) 날	But each ice skate has a blade.
2	each	각각(의)	Each in-line skate has four wheels in a line.
3	frozen	언, 얼어붙은	You can ice skate inside on rinks or outside on frozen lakes.
4	ground	지면, 땅바닥	You can in-line skate inside on rinks or outside on hard ground.
5	hard	단단한, 딱딱한	You can in-line skate inside on rinks or outside on hard ground.
6	ice skating	빙상 스케이트	Do you like in-line skating or ice skating?
7	inside	~의 안에	You can ice skate inside on rinks or outside on frozen lakes.
8	lake	호수	You can ice skate inside on rinks or outside on frozen lakes.
9	on	~ 위에	You can in-line skate inside on rinks or outside on hard ground.
10	outside	밖에, 외부에	You can ice skate inside on rinks or outside on frozen lakes.
11	rink	스케이트장	You can in-line skate inside on rinks or outside on hard ground.
12	wheel	바퀴	Each in-line skate has four wheels in a line.

Lesson 3 · What's for Breakfast?

	Vocabulary	Meaning	Sentence
1	common	흔한, 보통의	In France, toast with jam and croissants are common for breakfast.
2	famous	유명한	The famous American breakfast is thick pancakes with syrup and blueberries.
3	ground	빻은, 가루로 만든	People eat it plain or with ground meat.
4	meat	고기	People eat it plain or with ground meat.
5	people	사람들	People eat them with coffee or juice.
6	plain	담백한, 양념을 치지 않은	People eat it plain or with ground meat.
7	popular	인기 있는	Congee, a type of rice porridge, is a popular breakfast in China.
8	porridge	포리지 (오트밀 따위의 죽)	Congee, a type of rice porridge, is a popular breakfast in China.
9	thick	두꺼운, 두툼한	The famous American breakfast is thick pancakes with syrup and blueberries.
10	toast	토스트	In France, toast with jam and croissants are common for breakfast.
11	type	종류, 유형	Congee, a type of rice porridge, is a popular breakfast in China.
12	with	～와 함께	In France, toast with jam and croissants are common for breakfast.

Lesson 4 · Packing

	Vocabulary	Meaning	Sentence
1	dressed	옷을 입은 (잠옷 차림이 아닌)	Get dressed.
2	get	(어떤 상태가) 되다, 되게 하다	Get dressed.
3	hat*	모자	Did you pack your hat?
4	okay	네, 응, 좋아	Okay.
5	pack	(짐을) 싸다	Did you pack your pants?
6	pants*	바지	Did you pack your pants?
7	shirt*	셔츠	Did you pack your shirt?
8	socks*	양말	Did you pack your socks?
9	T-shirt*	티셔츠	Did you pack your T-shirt?
10	underwear*	속옷	Did you pack your underwear?
11	you	너, 당신	Did you pack your socks?
12	your	너의, 당신의	Did you pack your underwear?

Lesson 7 · Camping Items

	Vocabulary	Meaning	Sentence
1	are	～에 있다	We're here.
2	ball*	공	I brought a ball.
3	bring	가져오다	What did you bring?
4	flashlight*	손전등	I brought a flashlight.
5	garden spade*	정원용 삽	I brought a garden spade.
6	here	여기에	We're here.
7	hooray	만세 (즐거울 때)	Hooray!
8	jump rope*	줄넘기	I brought a jump rope.
9	raincoat*	비옷	I brought a raincoat.
10	umbrella*	우산	I brought an umbrella.
11	we	우리	We're here.
12	what	무엇	What did you bring?

Lesson 8 · Belongings

	Vocabulary	Meaning	Sentence
1	blanket*	담요	I forgot my blanket.
2	can	～해도 된다 (허가)	You can use my blanket.
3	cup*	컵, 잔	You can use my cup.
4	forgot	forget(잊어버리다)의 과거	I forgot my blanket.
5	my	나의	You can use my blanket.
6	pillow*	베개	You can use my pillow.
7	shampoo*	샴푸	You can use my shampoo.
8	soap*	비누	You can use my soap.
9	toothpaste*	치약	You can use my toothpaste.
10	use	쓰다, 사용하다	You can use my pillow.
11	worry	걱정하다	Don't worry.
12	wrong	(잘못된) 일이 있는, 이상이 있는	What's wrong?

Lesson 9 — You Can Use My Pillow

	Vocabulary	Meaning	Sentence
1	at	(시간) ~에	You need pajamas to wear at night.
2	friend	친구	When you go to a pajama party, you stay overnight at the home of a friend.
3	fun	재미, 즐거움	Now, let's have fun at a pajama party.
4	need	~을 필요로 하다	You need pajamas to wear at night.
5	overnight	하룻밤 동안	When you go to a pajama party, you stay overnight at the home of a friend.
6	pajamas	파자마, 잠옷	You need pajamas to wear at night.
7	pajama party	친구 집에 모여 밤새워 노는 모임	Now, let's have fun at a pajama party.
8	snack	간단한 간식	Don't forget some snacks.
9	some	조금, 약간의	Don't forget some snacks.
10	stay	머무르다	When you go to a pajama party, you stay overnight at the home of a friend.
11	watch	보다	You can play board games and watch movies with your friends.
12	wear	입고 있다	You need pajamas to wear at night.

Lesson 11 — Going Places

	Vocabulary	Meaning	Sentence
1	cave*	동굴	We're going to the cave.
2	fishing	낚시	Let's go fishing.
3	go to	~로 가다	We're going to the river.
4	great	굉장한, 아주 좋은	Sounds great.
5	mountain*	산	We're going to the mountains.
6	park*	공원	We're going to the park.
7	river*	강	We're going to the river.
8	sea*	바다	We're going to the sea.
9	sound	~처럼 들리다	Sounds great.
10	we	우리	Where are we going?
11	where	어디로	Where are we going?
12	zoo*	동물원	We're going to the zoo.

Lesson 14 — Games

	Vocabulary	Meaning	Sentence
1	a computer game*	컴퓨터 게임	Let's play a computer game.
2	basketball*	농구	Let's play basketball.
3	bingo*	빙고	Let's play bingo.
4	chess*	체스	Let's play chess.
5	hide and seek*	숨바꼭질	Let's play hide and seek.
6	let's	~하자	Let's play hide and seek.
7	play	(게임 · 놀이를) 하다, 놀다	What would you like to play?
8	soccer*	축구	Let's play soccer.
9	us	우리를, 우리에게	Play with us.
10	what	무엇	What would you like to play?
11	with	~와 함께	Play with us.
12	would like to	~하고 싶다	What would you like to play?

Lesson 15 — Dinnertime

	Vocabulary	Meaning	Sentence
1	careful	조심하는	Be careful using the knife.
2	dinner	저녁 식사	Will you help me with dinner?
3	fork*	포크	Be careful using the fork.
4	hammer*	망치	Be careful using the hammer.
5	help	돕다	Will you help me with dinner?
6	knife*	칼	Be careful using the knife.
7	pin*	압정	Be careful using the pin.
8	problem	문제	No problem.
9	scissors*	가위	Be careful using the scissors.
10	stove*	난로, 스토브	Be careful using the stove.
11	use	사용하다	Be careful using the knife.
12	will	~할 것이다	Okay, I will.

Lesson 12   Fishing

	Vocabulary	Meaning	Sentence
1	bigger*	더 큰 (big의 비교급)	This lemon is bigger than that one.
2	caught	catch(잡다)의 과거형	I caught one.
3	fish	물고기	This fish is bigger than that one.
4	heavier*	더 무거운 (heavy의 비교급)	This peach is heavier than that one.
5	lemon	레몬	This lemon is bigger than that one.
6	lighter*	더 가벼운 (light의 비교급)	This pear is lighter than that one.
7	longer*	더 긴 (long의 비교급)	This pencil is longer than that one.
8	orange	오렌지	This orange is smaller than that one.
9	peach	복숭아	This peach is heavier than that one.
10	pear	배	This pear is lighter than that one.
11	shorter*	더 짧은 (short의 비교급)	This pencil is shorter than that one.
12	smaller*	더 작은 (small의 비교급)	This orange is smaller than that one.

Lesson 13   Let's Go Fishing

	Vocabulary	Meaning	Sentence
1	beautiful	아름다운	You can take pictures of beautiful fish.
2	dive	(물속으로) 뛰어들다	Now, let's dive into the sea!
3	exercise	운동	You should do warm-up exercises before doing it.
4	fin	(물고기의) 지느러미	For snorkeling, you need a diving mask and fins.
5	life	생명, 삶	You can see amazing sea life under the sea.
6	mask	가면	For snorkeling, you need a diving mask and fins.
7	picture	사진, 그림	You can take pictures of beautiful fish.
8	see	보다	You can see amazing sea life under the sea.
9	sport	운동 경기	You can enjoy many water sports there.
10	there	거기에	You can enjoy many water sports there.
11	under	~아래에	You can see amazing sea life under the sea.
12	water	물	You can enjoy many water sports there.

Lesson 16   Will You Help Me with Dinner?

	Vocabulary	Meaning	Sentence
1	design	디자인, 설계	You can make various domino designs.
2	easy	쉬운	It's easy to do.
3	fall	떨어지다	The dominoes will fall down in order.
4	first	첫 번째	First, set up a line of dominoes.
5	knock	두드리다, 치다	Be careful not to knock down any dominoes when you make lines.
6	line	선, 줄	First, set up a line of dominoes.
7	order	순서	The dominoes will fall down in order.
8	second	두 번째	Second, tap the first domino.
9	set up	세우다	First, set up a line of dominoes.
10	tap	가볍게 두드리다	Second, tap the first domino.
11	topple	넘어뜨리다	Now, let's topple some dominoes!
12	various	다양한	You can make various domino designs.

Lesson 17   Campfire

	Vocabulary	Meaning	Sentence
1	could	can의 과거형 (부탁의 의미)	Could you play the harmonica?
2	excited	신이 난	Are you excited?
3	harmonica*	하모니카	Could you play the harmonica?
4	not	~않다	Sure, why not?
5	piano*	피아노	Could you play the piano?
6	play	(악기를) 연주하다	Could you play the harmonica?
7	sure	물론	Sure, why not?
8	tambourine*	탬버린	Could you play the tambourine?
9	trumpet*	트럼펫	Could you play the trumpet?
10	violin*	바이올린	Could you play the violin?
11	why	왜	Sure, why not?
12	xylophone*	실로폰	Could you play the xylophone?

Lesson 18   Shooting Star

	Vocabulary	Meaning	Sentence
1	amazing	놀라운	Amazing!
2	bike*	자전거	My wish is to get a new bike.
3	doll*	인형	My wish is to get a new doll.
4	get	얻다, 가지다	My wish is to get a new bike.
5	jacket*	재킷, 상의	My wish is to get a new jacket.
6	make	만들다	Let's make a wish.
7	new	새로운	My wish is to get a new bike.
8	robot*	로봇	My wish is to get a new robot.
9	shoot	쏘다, 휙 움직이다	Look at the shooting star.
10	soccer ball*	축구공	My wish is to get a new soccer ball.
11	watch*	시계	My wish is to get a new watch.
12	wish	소원	Let's make a wish.

Lesson 19   Are You Excited?

	Vocabulary	Meaning	Sentence
1	across	가로질러	They look like stars moving across the sky.
2	air	공기, 대기	They burn up in the air.
3	burn	불타다	They burn up in the air.
4	different	다른	But, actually, they are different from normal stars.
5	dust	먼지	A shooting star is a small piece of rock or dust.
6	glow	빛나다	When it falls down, it is hot and glowing.
7	move	움직이다	They look like stars moving across the sky.
8	normal	일반적인	But, actually, they are different from normal stars.
9	piece	조각	A shooting star is a small piece of rock or dust.
10	reach	~에 닿다, 도달하다	Most shooting stars don't reach the ground.
11	rock	바위, 돌	A shooting star is a small piece of rock or dust.
12	unlike	~와는 달리	Unlike shooting stars, normal stars don't fall and burn up quickly.

Memo

Memo

Answers

Student Book
Answers

Lesson 1 Greetings
B. Look, read, and choose.   p. 8
1. ⓓ   2. ⓒ   3. ⓑ   4. ⓐ

C. Match and say.   p. 9

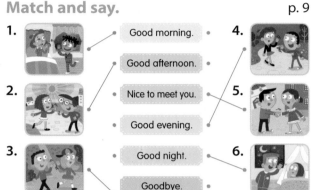

Lesson 2 Breakfast
B. Look, listen, and match.   p. 12

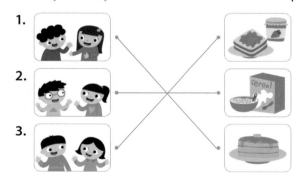

C. Check, ask, and answer.   p. 13
2. rice   3. salad   4. bread and jam
5. cereal   6. bacon and eggs

Lesson 3 What's for Breakfast?
B. Listen and number the pictures.   p. 14

C. Read and check True or False.   p. 15
1. False   2. True   3. True

Reading Time   p. 17
1. No. People around the world eat different foods.
2. The famous breakfast in America is thick pancakes with syrup and blueberries.

Lesson 4 Packing
B. Look, listen, and number the pictures. p. 20

C. Go down the ladder. Then, ask and answer.
p. 21

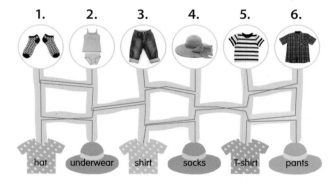

Lesson 5 Outdoor Activities
B. Look, read, and circle.   p. 24
1. camping, camping   2. hiking, hiking
3. fishing, fishing

C. Check, ask, and answer.   p. 25
2. hiking   3. jumping rope
4. in-line skating   5. camping   6. running

Lesson 6 I Love In-line Skating
B. Listen and number the pictures.   p. 26

C. Read and choose. p. 27

1. ⓑ   2. ⓐ

Reading Time p. 29

1. In-line skates have four wheels, and ice skates have blades.

2. I can in-line skate inside on rinks or outside on hard ground. I can ice skate inside on rinks or outside on frozen lakes.

Lesson 7 Camping Items

B. Look, read, and check. p. 32

1. I brought a flashlight.
2. I brought a garden spade.
3. I brought a raincoat.
4. I brought an umbrella.

C. Choose, ask, and answer. p. 33

2. ⓔ   3. ⓑ   4. ⓒ   5. ⓓ   6. ⓕ

D. Work with your friends. p. 33

Lesson 8 Belongings

B. Look, listen, and choose. p. 36

1. ⓐ   2. ⓑ   3. ⓑ   4. ⓐ

C. Match and say. p. 37

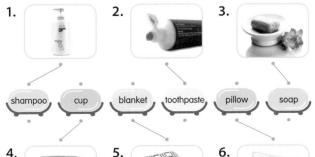

1. 2. 3.

shampoo   cup   blanket   toothpaste   pillow   soap

4.   5.   6.

Lesson 9 You Can Use My Pillow

B. Listen and number the pictures. p. 38

③   ①   ④   ②

C. Read and match. p. 39

1. ⓐ   2. ⓑ

Reading Time p. 41

1. I need pajamas to wear and some snacks.

2. I can play board games, watch movies, and eat snacks with my friends.

Lesson 10 Assessment Test 1

Listening p. 42

A. 1. b   2. a   3. b   4. b   5. a   6. a

B. 1. c   2. a

Speaking p. 43

A. 1. Yes, I did.   2. Okay.
   3. Yes, I love camping.
   4. I brought a flashlight.

B. ③ Don't worry. You can use my blanket.
   ② I forgot my blanket.
   ④ Thank you.

Reading p. 44

A. 1. e   2. c   3. b   4. f   5. a   6. d

B. 1. True   2. False   3. True

Writing p. 45

A. 1. fishing   2. underwear
   3. pillow   4. pancakes
   5. raincoat   6. in-line skating

B. 1. We have bacon and eggs.
   2. I forgot my blanket.
   3. I brought a flashlight.

Lesson 11 Going Places

B. Look, read, and match. p. 48

1. ⓑ   2. ⓐ   3. ⓓ   4. ⓒ

C. Choose, ask, and answer. p. 49

2. ⓔ   3. ⓐ   4. ⓑ   5. ⓕ   6. ⓓ

D. Work with your friends. p. 49

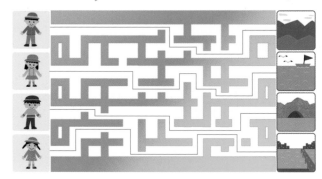

Lesson 12 Fishing

B. Look, listen, and check True or False. p. 52

1. False   2. True   3. True   4. False

C. Check and say. p. 53

2. smaller   3. longer   4. heavier
5. lighter   6. shorter

Lesson 13 Let's Go Fishing

B. Listen and number the pictures. p. 54

C. Read and choose. p. 55

1. ⓑ   2. ⓒ

Reading Time p. 57

1. I can see amazing sea life under the sea.
2. I need a diving mask and fins.

Lesson 14 Games

B. Look, listen, and number the pictures. p. 60

C. Go down the ladder. Then, ask and answer. p. 61

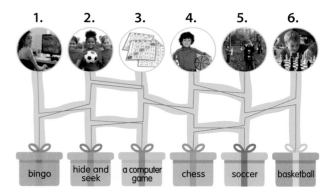

Lesson 15 Dinnertime

B. Look, read, and check. p. 64

1. Be careful using the hammer.
2. Will you help me with dinner?
3. Be careful using the scissors.
4. Be careful using the stove.

C. Match and say. p. 65

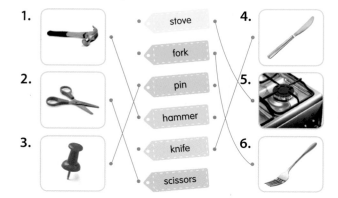

D. Work with your friends.   p. 65

Lesson 16   Will You Help Me with Dinner?

B. Listen and number the pictures.   p. 66

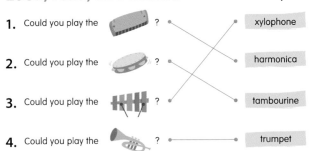

②   ④   ③   ①

C. Read and check True or False.   p. 67

1. True   **2.** False

Reading Time   p. 69

1. We should set up a line of dominoes.
2. We should be careful not to knock down any dominoes when we make lines.

Lesson 17   Campfire

B. Look, read, and match.   p. 72

1. Could you play the [harmonica] ? → xylophone
2. Could you play the [tambourine] ? → harmonica
3. Could you play the [xylophone] ? → tambourine
4. Could you play the [trumpet] ? → trumpet

C. Check, ask, and answer.   p. 73

2. violin   **3.** trumpet   **4.** piano

5. xylophone   **6.** harmonica

Lesson 18   Shooting Star

B. Look, listen, and choose.   p. 76

1. ⓐ   **2.** ⓑ   **3.** ⓑ   **4.** ⓑ

C. Choose and say.   p. 77

2. ⓒ   **3.** ⓕ   **4.** ⓑ   **5.** ⓐ   **6.** ⓔ

Lesson 19   Are You Excited?

B. Listen and number the pictures.   p. 78

③   ①   ④   ②

C. Read and correct the sentences.   p. 79

1. sad → excited   2. tambourine → violin
3. can't → can

Reading Time   p. 81

1. Normal stars don't fall and burn up quickly.
2. No. They burn up in the air.

Lesson 20   Assessment Test 2

Listening   p. 82

A. 1. b   **2.** a   **3.** a   **4.** b   **5.** b   **6.** a

B. 1. a   **2.** b

Speaking   p. 83

A. 1. No problem.
    2. Let's play hide and seek.
    3. Okay, I will. Thanks.
    4. My wish is to get a new robot.

B. ④ Yes, it is.
    ③ This fish is bigger than that one.
    ② I caught one, too.

Reading   p. 84

A. 1. c   **2.** a   **3.** e   **4.** f   **5.** d   **6.** b

B. 1. True   **2.** False   **3.** False

Writing   p. 85

A. 1. mountains   **2.** bingo
    3. robot   **4.** scissors
    5. xylophone   **6.** smaller

B. 1. We're going to the sea.
    2. Let's play hide and seek.
    3. My wish is to get a new bike.

Workbook
Answers

Lesson 1 Greetings
pp. 4~5

A. 1. morning 2. afternoon 3. evening 4. night

B. 1. It's Saturday.
2. Good morning, Mom.

C. Saturday camping
It's Saturday
Oh, it's camping day.

D. morning morning
1. afternoon afternoon
2. evening Good evening.
3. Good night. Good night.

Lesson 2 Breakfast
pp. 6~7

A. 1. cereal 2. bacon and eggs 3. bread and jam 4. pancakes

B. 1. It's sunny.
2. What's for breakfast?

C. ①
What's the weather like today?
It's sunny.

D. breakfast bacon and eggs
1. breakfast cereal
2. for breakfast have bread and jam
3. What's for breakfast?
We have pancakes.

Lesson 3 What's for Breakfast?
pp. 8~9

A. 1. morning 2. weather 3. Saturday 4. breakfast pancakes

B. 1. Good afternoon.
2. What's the weather like today?
3. Oh, it's camping day.
4. We have bacon and eggs.

Reading Time
1. toast
2. coffee
3. croissant
4. syrup

c	r	o	i	s	s	a	n	t
f	g	i	x	w	i	g	n	o
t	r	k	g	i	b	v	j	a
i	s	c	o	f	f	e	e	s
e	q	f	d	v	x	t	j	t
j	w	t	i	i	o	x	p	b
o	d	s	a	w	z	d	i	p
t	p	i	t	s	y	r	u	p
p	s	t	w	d	f	w	v	e

Lesson 4 Packing
pp. 10~11

A. 1. pants 2. socks 3. underwear 4. shirt

B. 1. Get dressed.
2. Did you pack your pants?

C. 1. Get dressed. 2. Okay.

D. socks did
1. pants did
2. pack your underwear I did
3. Did you pack your shirt? Yes, I did.

Lesson 5 Outdoor Activities
pp. 12~13

A. 1. hiking   2. in-line skating

3. fishing   4. camping

B. 1. Sorry for being late.

2. Teddy, do you like camping?

C. ②

Sorry for being late.

It's not a problem.

D. in-line skating   in-line skating

1. hiking   hiking

2. like camping   love camping

3. Do you like fishing?

Yes, I love fishing.

Lesson 6 I Love In-line Skating
pp. 14~15

A. 1. in-line skating   2. dressed

3. late   4. socks   did

B. 1. Do you like fishing?

2. Get dressed.

3. Sorry for being late.

4. Did you pack your shirt?

Reading Time

1. frozen   2. rink

3. wheel   4. lake

5. blade   6. ice skate

Lesson 7 Camping Items
pp. 16~17

A. 1. umbrella   2. raincoat

3. garden spade   4. flashlight

B. 1. We're here.

2. What did you bring?

C. here   Hooray

We're here.   Hooray!

D. bring   flashlight

1. bring   umbrella

2. you bring   a garden spade

3. What did you bring?

I brought a raincoat.

Lesson 8 Belongings
pp. 18~19

A. 1. blanket   2. pillow

3. shampoo   4. toothpaste

B. 1. I forgot my blanket.

2. You can use my blanket.

C. 1. What's wrong~~~~

→ What's wrong?

2. I forgot my shampoo.

→ I forgot my blanket.

D. pillow   Thank

1. toothpaste   Thank

2. use my blanket   Thank

3. You can use my shampoo.

Thank you.

Lesson 9 You Can Use My Pillow   pp. 20~21

A. 1. here   2. blanket

3. wrong   pillow

4. use

B. 1. We're here.

2. I brought a flashlight.

3. I forgot my blanket.

4. You can use my blanket.

Reading Time

1. party   2. home

3. pajamas   4. watch

Lesson 11 Going Places   pp. 22~23

A. 1. mountains   2. sea

3. cave   4. river

B. 1. Sounds great.

2. Where are we going?

C. fishing   great

Let's go fishing.   Sounds great.

D. going   river

1. we going   to the mountains

2. are we going   going to the cave

3. Where are we going?

3. We're going to the sea.

Lesson 12 Fishing   pp. 24~25

A. 1. smaller   2. bigger

3. lighter   4. heavier

B. 1. I caught one.

2. This fish is bigger than that one.

C. ②

I caught one.

I caught one, too.

D. bigger

1. bag   heavier   is

2. ball   smaller than   it is

3. bag is lighter than   Yes, it is.

Lesson 13 Let's Go Fishing   pp. 26~27

A. 1. great   2. Where   sea

3. caught   4. bigger

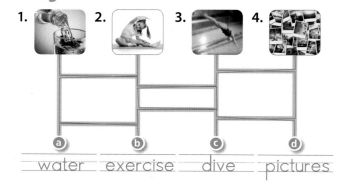

B. 1. Let's go fishing.

2. We're going to the mountains.

3. I caught one, too.

4. This ball is smaller than that one.

Reading Time

1.   2.   3.   4.

ⓐ   ⓑ   ⓒ   ⓓ

water   exercise   dive   pictures

Lesson 14 Games
pp. 28~29

A. 1. chess   2. bingo

    3. a computer game

    4. hide and seek

B. 1. Chris, play with us.

    2. What would you like to play?

C. ①

Play with us.   Okay.

D. play   bingo

    1. like to play   chess

    2. would you like to play

      play hide and seek

    3. What would you like to play?

      Let's play a computer game.

Lesson 15 Dinnertime
pp. 30~31

A. 1. hammer   2. scissors

    3. knife   4. stove

B. 1. No problem.

    2. Be careful using the knife.

C. 1. Will you play me with dinner?

     ➡ Will you help me with dinner?

    2. That's problem.

     ➡ No problem.

D. stove   Thanks.

    1. using the scissors   Thanks.

    2. careful using the knife

      I will. Thanks

    3. Be careful using the hammer.

      Okay. I will. Thanks.

Lesson 16 Will You Help Me with Dinner?
pp. 32~33

A. 1. problem   2. knife   3. Okay.

    4. What   hide and seek

B. 1. Will you help me with dinner?

    2. Be careful using the scissors.

    3. Play with us.

    4. Let's play a computer game.

Reading Time

1. dominoes

t	h	f	p	l	l	k	o	n
x	t	p	s	i	b	v	y	e
d	o	m	i	n	o	e	s	l
m	p	c	r	e	s	o	r	a
a	p	t	u	b	t	o	n	b
k	l	u	e	o	i	o	q	l
l	e	c	i	r	c	l	e	s
e	m	g	l	a	l	s	e	y

2. line

3. topple   4. circles

Lesson 17 Campfire
pp. 34~35

A. 1. tambourine   2. harmonica

    3. trumpet   4. xylophone

B. 1. Are you excited?

    2. Sure, why not?

C. Are   Yes

Are you excited?   Yes, I am.

D. harmonica

    1. tambourine   not

    2. play the xylophone   why not

    3. Could you play the trumpet?

      Sure, why not?

Lesson 18 Shooting Star　　pp. 36~37

A. 1. jacket　　2. watch
   3. robot　　4. bike

B. 1. Look at the shooting star.
   2. Let's make a wish.

C. 1. Look at the shooting star.
   2. Amazing!

D. wish　robot
   1. a wish　a new jacket
   2. make a wish　get a new bike
   3. Let's make a wish.
      wish is to get a new watch

Lesson 19 Are You Excited?　　pp. 38~39

A. 1. excited　　2. Amazing
   3. make　wish　　4. why

B. 1. Are you excited?
   2. Look at the shooting star.
   3. My wish is to get a new watch.
   4. Could you play the trumpet?

Reading Time

1. stars　　2. rock
3. dust　　4. burn

Final Test
English Town Book 1

1. ②	2. ⑤	3. ③	4. ②	5. ④
6. ①	7. ③	8. ④	9. ①	10. ④
11. ④	12. ③	13. ②	14. ①	15. ④
16. ③	17. ⑤	18. ②		

19. fishing　　20. harmonica

ENGLiSH TOWN

FOR EVERYONE

BOOK 1

WORKBOOK

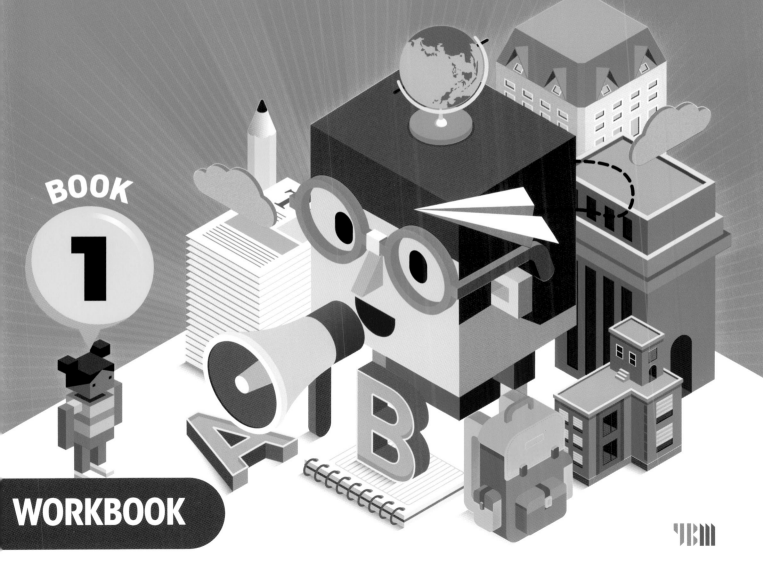

YBM

ENGLISH TOWN

FOR EVERYONE

BOOK

1

WORKBOOK

Contents

1 Greetings

Let's Write

A. Write the words.

① ② ③ ④

_____ _____ _____ _____

evening   morning   night   afternoon

B. Choose and write.

*C: Chris   R: Rachel   RM: Rachel's Mom

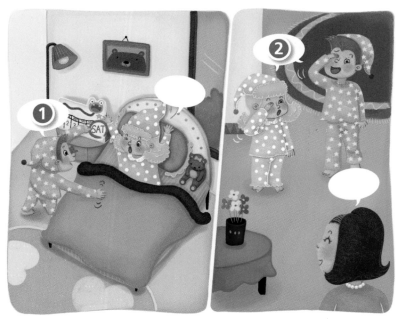

① C: _____

R: Oh, it's camping day.

② R,C: _____

RM: Good morning.

• Good morning, Mom.
• It's Saturday.

C. Look and fill in the blanks.

A: It's _____ .

B: Oh, it's _____ day.

• **Write the sentences.**

A: _____   B: _____

D. Look and write.

Example

A: Good morning .

B: Good morning .

①

A: Good _____ .

B: Good _____ .

②

A: Good _____ .

B: _____ .

③

A: _____ .

B: _____ .

2 Breakfast

Let's Write

A. Write the words.

①

②

③

④

○ bread and jam   pancakes   bacon and eggs   cereal ○

B. Choose and write.

*R: Rachel   RD: Rachel's Dad   C: Chris   RM: Rachel's Mom

① RD: What's the weather like today?

R:

② C:

RM: We have cereal.

- It's sunny.
- What's for breakfast?

C. Look and choose.

1. A: What's the weather like today?
   B: It's sunny.

2. A: Good night.
   B: Good night.

- **Write the sentences.**

A: _____

B: _____

D. Look and write.

Example

A: What's for breakfast ?

B: We have bacon and eggs .

1.

   A: What's for _____ ?

   B: We have _____ .

2.

   A: What's _____ ?

   B: We _____ .

3.

   A: _____

   B: _____

3 What's for Breakfast?

Let's Write

A. Write the words and number the pictures.

1 Dodo: Good morning.

Dodo's Dad: Good _____, Dad.

2 Dodo: What's the _____ like today?

Dodo's Dad: It's sunny.

3 Dodo's Dad: It's _____.

Dodo: Oh, it's my birthday.

4 Dodo: What's for _____?

Dodo's Mom: We have _____.

weather

breakfast

Saturday

morning

pancakes

B. Unscramble and complete the dialogs.

1 A: _____

(afternoon / good / .)

B: Good afternoon.

2 A: _____

(the / weather / today / like / what's / ?)

B: It's sunny.

3 A: It's Saturday.

B: _____

(day / it's / camping / oh, / .)

4 A: What's for breakfast?

B: _____

(have / bacon and eggs / we / .)

Reading Time

- **Find the words and write.**

1

_____

3

_____

c	r	o	i	s	s	a	n	t
f	g	i	x	w	i	g	n	o
t	r	k	g	i	b	v	j	a
i	s	c	o	f	f	e	e	s
e	q	f	d	v	x	t	j	t
j	w	t	i	i	o	x	p	b
o	d	s	a	w	z	d	i	p
t	p	i	t	s	y	r	u	p
p	s	t	w	d	f	w	v	e

2

_____

4

_____

4 Packing

Let's Write

A. Write the words.

① ② ③ ④

socks   pants   shirt   underwear

B. Choose and write.

*RD: Rachel's Dad   R: Rachel   C: Chris

① RD: _____

R: Okay.

② RD: _____

C: Yes, I did.

- Did you pack your pants?
- Get dressed.

C. Reorder the letters in the boxes and complete the sentences.

① Get [r e d s s d e] .

➡ _____

② [k y a o] .

➡ _____

D. Look and write.

Example

A: Did you pack your ___socks___ ?

B: Yes, I ___did___ .

① A: Did you pack your _____ ?

B: Yes, I _____ .

② A: Did you _____ ?

B: Yes, _____ .

③ A: _____

B: _____

5 Outdoor Activities

Let's Write

A. Write the words.

① ② ③ ④

| fishing | camping | hiking | in-line skating |

B. Choose and write.

*TD: Teddy's Dad   RD: Rachel's Dad   T: Teddy

① TD: _____

RD: It's not a problem.

② RD: _____

T: Yes, I love camping.

- Sorry for being late.
- Teddy, do you like camping?

C. Look and choose.

1 A: It's Saturday.
B: Oh, it's camping day.

2 A: Sorry for being late.
B: It's not a problem.

- **Write the sentences.**

A: _____   B: _____

D. Look and write.

Example

A: Do you like _in-line skating_ ?

B: Yes, I love _in-line skating_ .

1

A: Do you like _____ ?

B: Yes, I love _____ .

2

A: Do you _____ ?

B: Yes, I _____ .

3

A: _____

B: _____

6 I Love In-line Skating

Let's Write

A. **Write the words and number the pictures.**

1. Dodo's Mom: Do you like _____ ?

   Dodo: Yes, I love in-line skating.

2. Dodo's Mom: Get _____ .

   Dodo: Okay.

3. Dodo: Sorry for being _____ .

   Rubi: It's not a problem.

4. Rubi: Did you pack your _____ ?

   Dodo: Yes, I _____ .

dressed

did

socks

late

in-line skating

B. Unscramble and complete the dialogs.

1 A: _____

(you / fishing / do / like / ?)

B: Yes, I love fishing.

2 A: _____

(dressed / get / .)

B: Okay.

3 A: _____

(for / sorry / late / being / .)

B: It's not a problem.

4 A: _____

(pack / shirt /did / you / your / ?)

B: Yes, I did.

Reading Time

- **Choose and write the words.**

1 _____

2 _____

3 _____

4 _____

5 _____

6 _____

lake

blade

rink

ice skate

frozen

wheel

Camping Items

Let's Write

A. Write the words.

① ② ③ ④

umbrella   flashlight   garden spade   raincoat

B. Choose and write.

*TD: Teddy's Dad   E: Everyone   R: Rachel   T: Teddy

① TD: _____

E: Hooray!

② R: _____

T: I brought an umbrella.

• What did you bring?
• We're here.

C. Look and fill in the blanks.

A: We're _____ .

B: _____ !

- **Write the sentences.**

A: _____

B: _____

D. Look and write.

Example

A: What did you bring ?

B: I brought a flashlight .

①

A: What did you _____ ?

B: I brought an _____ .

②

A: What did _____ ?

B: I brought _____ .

③

A: _____

B: _____

Belongings

Let's Write

A. Write the words.

① ② ③ ④

pillow   shampoo   toothpaste   blanket

B. Choose and write.

*T: Teddy   C: Chris

① T: What's wrong?

C:

② T: Don't worry.

C: Thank you.

• I forgot my blanket.
• You can use my blanket.

C. Find mistakes and correct.

1 What's wrong.

➡ _____

2 I forgot my shampoo.

➡ _____

D. Look and write.

Example

A: Don't worry. You can use my _pillow_ .

B: _Thank_ you.

1

A: Don't worry. You can use my _____ .

B: _____ you.

2

A: Don't worry. You can _____ .

B: _____ you.

3

A: Don't worry. _____

B: _____

You Can Use My Pillow

Let's Write

A. Write the words and number the pictures.

① Bebe: We're _____ .
_____ .

Roy: Hooray!

② Dodo: What did you bring?

Bebe: I brought a _____ .
_____ .

③ Dodo: What's _____ ?
_____ ?

Bebe: I forgot my _____ .
_____ .

④ Dodo: Don't worry. You can _____ my pillow.
_____ my pillow.

Bebe: Thank you.

blanket

wrong

pillow

use

here

B. Unscramble and complete the dialogs.

1 A: _____

(here / we're / .)

B: Hooray!

2 A: What did you bring?

B: _____

(flashlight / brought / I / a / .)

3 A: What's wrong?

B: _____

(forgot / my / I / blanket / .)

4 A: Don't worry. _____

(can / you / my / use / blanket / .)

B: Thank you.

Reading Time

- **Break the codes and write.**

	1	2	3	4	5
1	a	j	p	h	t
2	o	c	e	r	y
3	s	g	i	w	m

Example
◆3 ☆2 △1 ◆2
→ wear

1  ☆1 △1 ◆2 ◎1 ◎2

2  ◆1 △2 ◎3 ☆2

3 ☆1 △1 □1 △1 ◎3 △1 △3

4 ◆3 △1 ◎1 □2 ◆1

11 Going Places

Let's Write

A. Write the words.

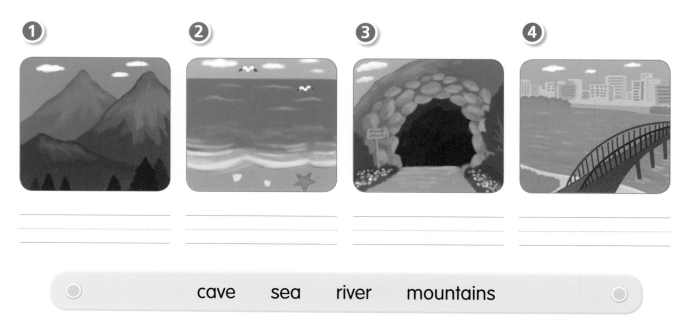

① ② ③ ④

cave   sea   river   mountains

B. Choose and write.

*TD: Teddy's Dad   RD: Rachel's Dad   R: Rachel   T: Teddy

① TD: Let's go fishing.

RD: _____

② R: _____

T: We're going to the river.

• Where are we going?
• Sounds great.

C. Look and fill in the blanks.

A: Let's go _____ .

B: Sounds _____ .

- **Write the sentences.**

A: _____

B: _____

D. Look and write.

Example

A: Where are we _going_ ?

B: We're going to the _river_ .

1

A: Where are _____ ?

B: We're going _____ .

2

A: Where _____ ?

B: We're _____ .

3

A: _____

B: _____

12 Fishing

Let's Write

A. Write the words.

① ② ③ ④

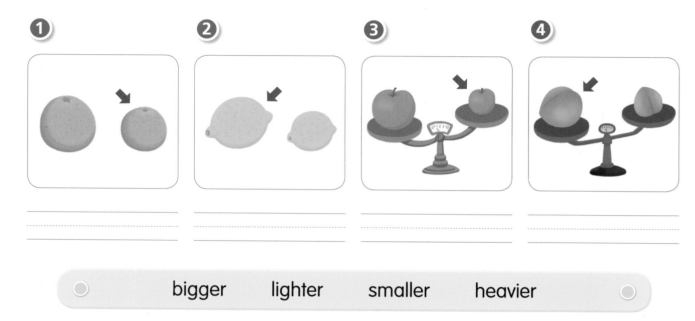

bigger   lighter   smaller   heavier

B. Choose and write.

* RD: Rachel's Dad   TD: Teddy's Dad   T: Teddy   R: Rachel

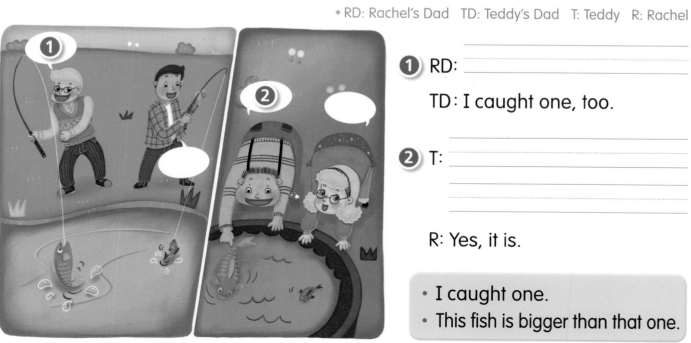

① RD: _____

TD : I caught one, too.

② T: _____

R: Yes, it is.

- I caught one.
- This fish is bigger than that one.

C. Look and choose.

① A: Let's go fishing.
B: I'm sorry.

② A: I caught one.
B: I caught one, too.

• **Write the sentences.**

A: _____   B: _____

D. Look and write.

Example

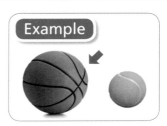

A: This ball is ___bigger___ than that one.

B: Yes, it is.

①

A: This _____ is _____ than that one.

B: Yes, it _____.

②

A: This _____ is _____ that one.

B: Yes, _____.

③

A: This _____ that one.

B: _____

13 Let's Go Fishing

Let's Write

A. Write the words and number the pictures.

① Bebe's Dad: Let's go fishing.

Bebe, Dodo: Sounds _____ .

② Bebe: _____ are we going?

Bebe's Dad: We're going to the _____ .

③ Bebe: I _____ one.

Dodo: I caught one, too.

④ Bebe: This fish is _____ than that one.

Dodo: Yes, it is.

bigger

sea

where

great

caught

B. Unscramble the words and complete the dialogs.

❶ A: _____

(go / let's / fishing / .)

B: Sounds great.

❷ A: Where are we going?

B: _____

(mountains / to / the / going / we're / .)

❸ A: I caught one.

B: _____

(I / too / , / one / caught / .)

❹ A: _____

(that / this / ball / one / smaller / is / than / .)

B: Yes, it is.

Reading Time

- **Do ghost leg and write the words.**

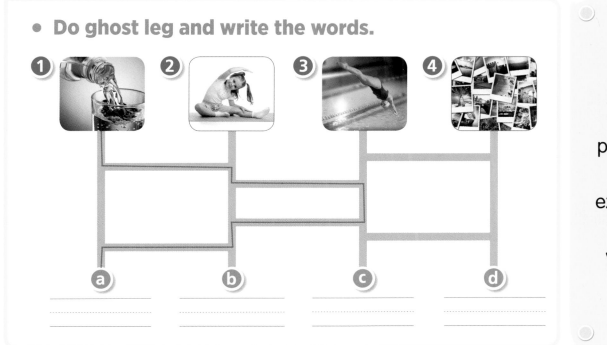

dive

pictures

exercise

water

a: _____ b: _____ c: _____ d: _____

14 Games

Let's Write

A. Write the words.

①

②

③

④

_____

_____

_____

_____

a computer game   chess   hide and seek   bingo

B. Choose and write.

*R: Rachel   C: Chris   T: Teddy

① R: _____

C: Okay.

② C: _____

_____

T: Let's play hide and seek.

• What would you like to play?
• Chris, play with us.

C. Look and choose.

1 A: Play with us.
B: Okay.

2 A: This ball is bigger than that one.
B: Yes, it is.

- **Write the sentences.**

A: _____

B: _____

D. Look and write.

Example

A: What would you like to play ?

B: Let's play bingo .

1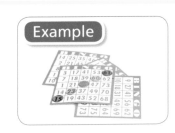

A: What would you _____?

B: Let's play _____.

2

A: What _____?

B: Let's _____.

3

A: _____

B: _____

Dinnertime

Let's Write

A. Write the words.

1 _____

2 _____

3 _____

4 _____

knife   scissors   stove   hammer

B. Choose and write.

*RM: Rachel's Mom   R: Rachel   TD: Teddy's Dad   T: Teddy

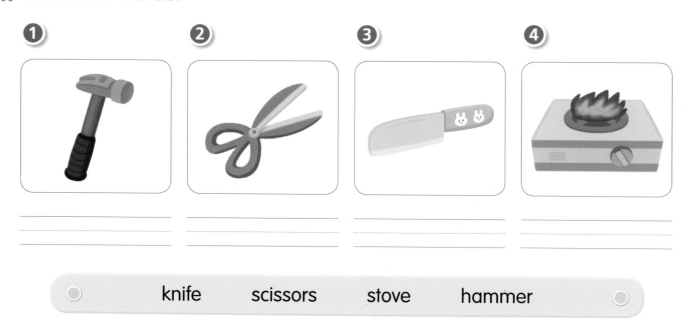

1 RM: Will you help me with dinner?

R: _____

2 TD: _____

T: Okay, I will. Thanks.

- No problem.
- Be careful using the knife.

C. Find mistakes and correct.

1 Will you play me with dinner?

➡ _____

2 That's problem.

➡ _____

D. Look and write.

A: Be careful using the _stove_ .

B: Okay, I will. _Thanks_____

Example

1

A: Be careful _____.

B: Okay, I will. _____

2

A: Be _____.

B: Okay, _____.

3

A: _____

B: _____

Will You Help Me with Dinner?

Let's Write

A. Write the words and number the pictures.

1 Dodo's Mom: Will you help me with dinner?

Dodo, Rubi: No _____.

2 Dodo's Dad: Be careful using the _____.

Rubi: Okay, I will. Thanks.

3 Dodo: Dad, play with us.

Dodo's Dad: _____

4 Dodo's Dad: _____ would you like to play?

Rubi: Let's play _____.

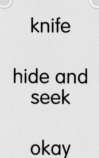

knife

hide and seek

okay

what

problem

B. **Unscramble the words and complete the dialogs.**

① A: _____

(will / with / help / you / me / dinner / ?)

B: No problem.

② A: _____

(scissors / using / careful / the / be / .)

B: Okay, I will. Thanks.

③ A: _____

(us / with / play / .)

B: Okay.

④ A: What would you like to play?

B: _____

(play / a / game / computer / let's / .)

Reading Time

- **Find out the words.**

①

d_____

③

t_____

t	h	f	p	l	l	k	o	n
x	t	p	s	i	b	v	y	e
d	o	m	i	n	o	e	s	l
m	p	c	r	e	s	o	r	a
a	p	t	u	b	t	o	n	b
k	l	u	e	o	i	o	q	l
l	e	c	i	r	c	l	e	s
e	m	g	l	a	l	s	e	y

②

l_____

④

c_____

Let's Write

A. Write the words.

① ② ③ ④

xylophone   tambourine   harmonica   trumpet

B. Choose and write.

*TM: Teddy's Mom   T: Teddy   R: Rachel   RD: Rachel's Dad

① TM: _____

T: Yes, I am.

② R: Could you play the harmonica?

RD: _____

• Sure, why not?
• Are you excited?

C. Look and fill in the blanks.

A: _____ you excited?

B: _____ , I am.

• **Write the sentences.**

A: _____

B: _____

D. Look and write.

Example

A: Could you play the harmonica ?

B: Sure, why not?

1

A: Could you play the _____ ?

B: Sure, why _____ ?

2

A: Could you _____ ?

B: Sure, _____ ?

3

A: _____

B: _____

18 Shooting Star

Let's Write

A. Write the words.

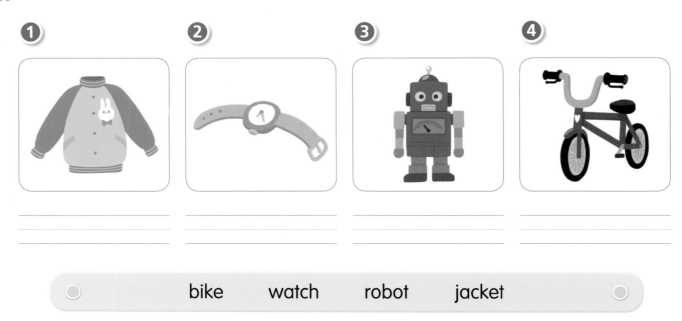

| ❶ | ❷ | ❸ | ❹ |

| bike | watch | robot | jacket |

B. Choose and write.

*RM: Rachel's Mom   E: Everyone   R: Rachel   T: Teddy

❶ RM: _____

E: Amazing!

❷ R: _____

T: My wish is to get a new bike.

- Let's make a wish.
- Look at the shooting star.

C. Reorder the letters in the boxes and complete the sentences.

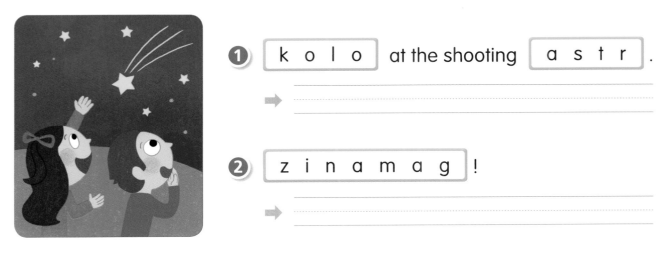

① `k o l o` at the shooting `a s t r` .

➡ _____

② `z i n a m a g` !

➡ _____

D. Look and write.

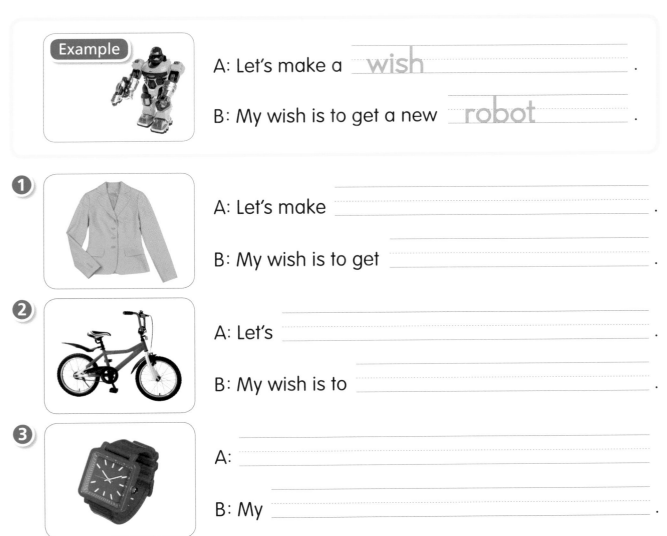

Example

A: Let's make a ___wish___ .

B: My wish is to get a new ___robot___ .

① A: Let's make _____ .

B: My wish is to get _____ .

② A: Let's _____ .

B: My wish is to _____ .

③ A: _____ .

B: My _____ .

Are You Excited?

Let's Write

A. Write the words and number the pictures.

1 Dodo's Dad: Are you _____?

Dodo: Yes, I am.

2 Dodo's Mom: Look at the shooting star.

Dodo: _____!

3 Dodo's Dad: Let's _____ a wish.

Dodo: My _____ is to get a new violin.

4 Dodo's Mom: Could you play the violin?

Dodo: Sure, _____ not?

amazing

wish

why

make

excited

B. **Unscramble the words and complete the dialogs.**

① A: _____

(you / excited / are / ?)

B: Yes, I am.

② A: _____

(star / shooting / look / the / at / .)

B: Amazing!

③ A: Let's make a wish.

B: _____

(a / wish / get / new / my / watch / to / is / .)

④ A: _____

(you / the / trumpet / could / play / ?)

B: Sure, why not?

Reading Time

- **Write the words.**

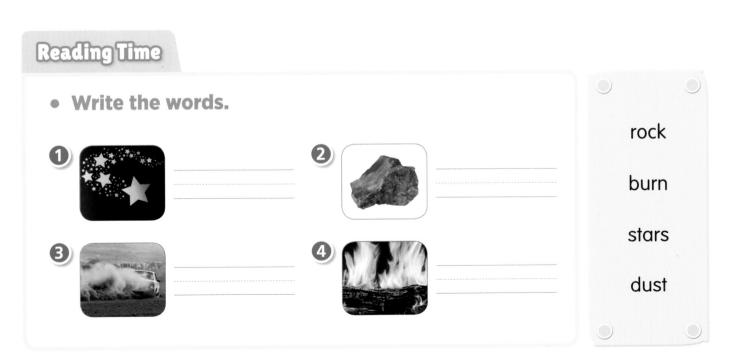

①

②

③

④

rock

burn

stars

dust

Memo

ENGLiSH TOWN

ENGLiSH TOWN BOOK 1

English Town is a spoken English course comprised of a series of 9 books, specifically designed for elementary school students.

- Learning English in a communicative way and in an easy manner
- Focused approach to new words, expressions, and dialogs
- Fun to sing and chant together
- Simple but effective games and activities
- Exciting stories

Components

· Student Book

· Workbook

· Final Test

· Teacher's Guide including teaching resources

· Online (www.ybmenglishtown.com)

  Interactive e-book for teachers and students

  E-learning for self-study

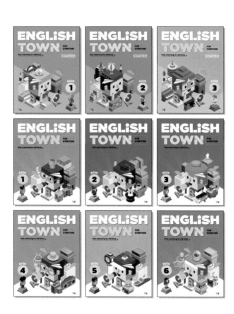

 www.ybmenglishtown.com

YBM